THE CHOCOLATE SWORD

Also by John Groves:

Fiction:
The Carapace

Poetry and Prose:
Naked Heaven, Naked Earth
   - An Environmental Philosophy
Poetry on Purpose

THE CHOCOLATE SWORD

John Groves

UNITED WRITERS
Cornwall

UNITED WRITERS PUBLICATIONS LTD
Ailsa, Castle Gate, Penzance, Cornwall.

British Library Cataloguing in Publication Data:
A catalogue record for this book is
available from the British Library.

ISBN 1 85200 064 3

Printed in Great Britain by
United Writers Publications Ltd
Cornwall.

For my friends

FOREWORD

In an earlier plan, *Good-Natured* or *Well-Tempered Giants* was to have been the title of the book, chosen to reassure friends who had come to associate me with 'doom-'n'-gloom'. That was certainly the general tenor of *Poetry on Purpose*, the anthology immediately preceding this.

A particular friend and neighbour observed that, for one who appears cheerful enough in everyday life, 'a vein of melancholy' runs through my previously published work. I suppose I commonly practise an innocent deception, putting a face on things braver than I feel, for I entertain a profound conviction that, through its own impenitent folly, the human race is stampeding toward oblivion.

But age has brought with it certain compensations and I have softened a little, to the extent that the title finally settled upon is a kind of compromise. With certain exceptions, the present work sounds a relatively cheerful - even optimistic - note . . . something like the songs sung on the *Titanic* as the ship went down!

J.G.
Barbican,
London, 1996

The Chocolate Sword
That, whether thrust
Or merely point toward,
Offers a sweetness as its rich reward,
But which must
Always remind how otherwise would feel,
Made of fierce-tempered steel
Impolitic, instead of good accord.

Walk tall and boldly,
Yet look not coldly
Upon your enemy,
But smile,
That he may be
Your Friend in a little while.

CONTENTS

Page

ACKNOWLEDGEMENTS

Much of the research for the poem about Giants was carried out in the City of London's Guildhall Library, coincidentally the site of extant effigies of Gog and Magog. I relied largely on material published early this century. However, my approach to it was wary, since mistakes perpetuated in more recently published work by other authors often derive from errors made in earlier works. The validity of what sometimes appears to be fact has duped many a scribe into believing in the verity of detail simply because it appeared to be corroborated elsewhere.

One particular howler - still perpetuated by those who ought to know better - confuses two quite different giants, Charles Byrne and Patrick Cotter O'Brien, whose only similarity rested upon their being Irish and broadly contemporary. There was, moreover, a difference of a good few inches in their respective heights, although they did, in point of fact, meet with similar fates.

I cannot say I fell under the spell of any one particular book, ancient or modern, but readily ascribe the idea of including one example of a giant who suffered from 'daddy-long-legs syndrome' to the useful and largely reliable summary published in the *Guinness Book of Records*, which makes up in accuracy what it lacks in comprehensiveness.

Wherever I have myself indulged in exaggerated claims, particularly in regard to height, it has been done deliberately and in an appropriately mocking way and without intention of misleading myself or any reader.

In that regard, I now regret not having included reference to Guy of Warwick, an English knight of legend and romance who reportedly slew several giants in the Holy Land before returning to Winchester, there to slay the evil Danish giant Colbrand, thus sparing England from paying Danish tribute. Guy is said to have been something of a giant himself. I understand there is 12th century manuscript that says so and 14th century ones that confirm it.

Despite that, I am content that my 20th century narrative confines itself to giants - not to giant-killers.

Advocates of metrication are reminded that the giants referred to were, in their day, measured in feet and inches. Purists who wish to make their own conversion may welcome reassurance that one foot equals 0.3048 metres exactly.

Illustrations

A painstaking search for illustrations only became rewarding when by good chance I made contact with Ms Angela Roche, of the British Museum's Department of Prints and Drawings, and with Mrs Henrietta Ryan, Deputy Curator of the Royal Library's Print Room at Windsor Castle.

It is to the former that I owe the much-coveted engraving by the 18th century sculptor Van Assen, representing my favourite giant, Patrick Cotter O'Brien. Until Ms. Roche's patient intervention, it had lain (like the giant himself) long mislaid. To Mrs Ryan I am indebted for a wealth of information about related engravings in the Royal Library; but for her, I would never have known that one of the shorter-sized figures who looked up to Henry Blacker so admiringly was no less than King George III. It is to Ms Roche again, and her colleagues, that I owe that print and two others, Rowlandson's as well as Van Assen's independent representations of the aforementioned Cotter O'Brien. The latter is seen here on the cover.

My thanks also to the long-lost artist of prehistory who conceived Dorsetshire's magnificent Cerne Abbas chalk giant, shyly represented herein, and the unknown creator of the remaining illustration gratefully included.

GOOD-NATURED GIANTS

'But really I'm not a monster.
I just happen to have grown terribly tall.'

Just as olde map tracks for waggons
Sometimes cautioned *Here bee Dragons*,
Others, showing greater pliance,
Might have added *Also Giants*.

For this story starts in misty
Times of myth and legend. Hist'ry
Too, but that came later still,
As you shall see, if you've a will.

Some say 'twas a time when the earth had three moons,
Two suns, sixteen seasons, five mornings, four Junes
And since everything grew at astonishing pace,
For a man to be monstrous was not a disgrace.

Legend quotes Genesis, which anciently says
Quite clear *there were giants in the earth in those days:*

In Rouen, France, they once did claim
A *seventeen-footer* there had lain;
But there's no-one of giant-addiction
Moved to sort the fact from fiction.

Some giants, we're told, could hurl a giant stone;
'Tis said we had a couple of our own:
Cornwall's Cormoran and Cornelian count -
The stones *they* threw we call St. Michael's Mount!

Colossal ten and twelve feet specimens of long ago,
Like legendary Goliath, many more we do not know.
What's certain is that giants all standard sizes did outpace.
One might describe them as sequoias of the human race.
No one is really certain just how big the giants were then;
Few traces from prehistory survive within our ken.
Like dinosaurs and Early Man and mammoths and old camels,
Their bones were eaten, when they died, by smaller kinds of mammals.

Arthurian wizard Merlin it is said was giant-sized
And massive feats, like circles of stone monoliths, devised.
Pliny wrote of Gabbarus, whose height was nine feet plus:
The tallest swain during the reign of the Emperor Claudius.
St. Christopher, once patron saint of travellers, 'tis said,
Was roughly eight feet something from his toes up to his head;
Andronicus the Second, a striking Byzantine,
Claimed to be some ten feet three (or was it eight feet nine?)
The Emperor Charlemagne's power and very warlike reputation
Exaggerated him to several feet above his station.

In Albion, tradition says a monster dynasty
Was spawned by an Emperor's daughters, in number thirty-three.
In fits of pique - which early speak of Women's Liberation -
They thought they'd like to found a female-dominated nation,
So murdered all their husbands and then for punishment
Were set adrift and foundered on the English coast of Kent.

And there they met some Englishmen of an eccentric mind
Who married them and gave them sons of quite titanic kind.
Ungodly, these alliances, unlucky they were, too,
For every giant they bore would come to meet his Waterloo.
Just two, called Gog and Magog, survived to tell the tale,
Chained and brought to London Town, where, being strong and hale,
They served as Palace porters, with determination gritty,
On what is now the Guildhall site in London's ancient City.

A sweeping change had come about throughout each foreign land
Where cruel Time gave to the Small the Mighty Upper Hand.
For overseas 'twas not a lucky thing to be born huge,
Inspiring terror, giants were there obliged to take refuge
In isolated forests, where they might be left alone
And no-one came to make their name, a-hurling stick or stone.
Endangered species, giants were then, living in mortal fear,
For little folk thought giants were not entitled to be here.

A point I'm anxious to attest
Is that, although they were the best,
Not all giants were of English birth.

14

That's no detraction from their worth.
The point I make is simply that
England became their habitat,
For there, preferred to all, it seems,
They found the country of their dreams.
There they did not have to shirk
The right to live and love and work.
They faced much curiosity,
But rarely animosity,
So feared no cruel retribution,
Choosing to make a contribution;
While, being eccentric, easily passed
As English, leaving none aghast.

Which brings us to a year of grace,
Four hundred years ago,
When giants from many kinds of place
Chose here a base to stow.
For this was when your genuine, undisputed giant arrived,
To be observed and listed, measured, weighed and codified.
Gentlemen of fortune, some; others simply porters,
Some became domestics serving wealthy mums and daughters
And towed around for every gaping hound in turn to see,
Tricked out with social pomp in rich and stylish livery.

Many suffered the unhappy fate of public recognition
As fairground curiosities, with freaks of all condition.
Managers, promoters knew a good thing when they saw it,
For when a giant is on display nobody can ignore it.
Vital measurements were often very much improved upon
And many an inch was added, many ounces to the ton.

(Rivals, anxious to outdo,
Added a further inch or two;
Others to earn a richer fee
Added an extra inch or *three*.)

Sometimes deplorable deceptions, boldly carried out,
Were with the giant's connivance, no law was deemed to flout,
For it was a simple way in which to earn an extra crust,
Since giant appetites demand that . . . when you must you must.

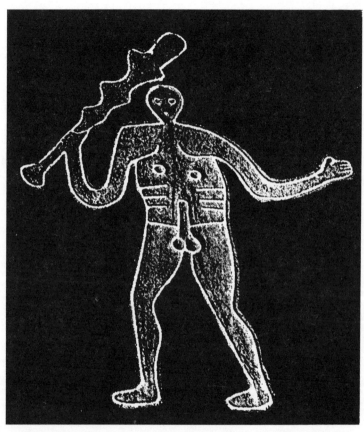

This chalk giant, of prehistoric origin, cut in the side of a hill at
Cerne Abbas, Dorsetshire, is in an earlier tradition of English
giants, symbolising potency and menace.

The only things had Cromwell and King Charles the First the same
Were porters so gigantic it earned each of them much fame.
The King's was William Evans - the cause of much ado
Being eight feet something when he died in Sixteen Thirty Two.

Cromwell's giant porter, Daniel,
Seven feet six and so no spaniel,
Height recorded so's to last till
Domesday, wall of Windsor Castle.
Daniel got religion badly;
Ended up in Bedlam, sadly,
Given, 'fore being taken in,
A king-sized Bible by Nell Gwynne.

A favourite of collectors was Cornelius Magrath,
An orphan lad adopted to augment a Bishop's hearth.
Bishop Berkeley had a fancy to succeed by science or art
In increasing human stature; with this orphan made a start,
Poor child convenient subject for a black experiment -
A thing for which no orphan boy should ever have been meant.
Some seven feet eight or seven feet ten was he by age sixteen
And died in Seventeen Sixty, his twenties barely seen,
For in the end he got a good deal less than he deserved:
His skeleton is one of several privately preserved.

Seven feet four and not contortioned -
Really awfully well proportioned -
Came in Seventeen Fifty-Two
Cuckfield's Henry Blacker who
Made London gasp with stupefaction:
'*Universal satisfaction . . .*
Seen in a commodious room
In Half-Moon Court', the posters boom.

Seven feet six, with more to gain,
Came Cornwall's giant Tony Payne;
A Royalist supporter, more,
Who fought in England's Civil War.
His reputation quite untainted,
King Charles had his portrait painted.

Rowlandson's 1785 cartoon of Patrick Cotter O'Brien calls his subject 'The Surprising Irish Giant of St. James's Street', which he was indeed, being in excess of 8 feet in height and a celebrated curiosity of London society.

It's my sincere conviction that most often giants died young.
Was it abnormality or 'coz of cruel tongue?
An Irish Giant, Charles Byrne, was seven feet eight - not less was he -
Who died when only twenty-two in Seventeen Eighty-Three.
The Surgeons' Royal College, in London's Lincoln's Inn,
Was quick to snap him up to store his skeleton within.
I say that this was not a fate he relished in his time
And carving up poor giants in my opinion is a crime.

Another giant Irishman, but durable as lion,
Was handsome, well-proportioned Patrick Cotter (called O'Brien).
Seventeen Sixty was alleged to be his year of birth,
The finest he of all the giants, for what my money's worth.
A one-time bricklayer, 'twas claimed that he was eight feet seven,
With all the attributes that could be granted him by heaven.
If truth be told he was more likely eight feet two, I guess,
Contemporary records say he could not have been less.

Given he was not unwilling,
More than justified his billing.
Manly, yet with winsome frilling,
Knew how to turn an honest shilling.
His height being such (much more than most)
Could light his pipe at a lamp-post.

The show circuit of London celebrated him in rhyme.
The ceilings of society were tallish at the time:
I've seen a picture of him - no gathering could ignore -
With elbow rested lightly on the top of someone's door!
How odd that we've forgotten such marvels did appear
On the stage at Sadlers Wells and at Bartholomew's great Fayre.

Here I will pause to say why giants so often feared to die:
It was because they knew that, soon as life had passed them by,
A surgeon lay in wait to flay the flesh from every bone,
Their private parts and skeletons would not be left alone!
Organs would be bottled up in strong formaldehyde,
That rubbernecking quacks might in their morbid trade be plied.

The kinky and the quirky then enjoyed a festive day
Discov'ring if what gossip said was true and not hearsay.

Before he died and in the pride of life at forty-six,
Cotter planned to quite withstand the stickybeaks their tricks.
He urged some Bristol friends to bury him so deep, 'tis said
The coffin measured nine feet two, made basically of lead,
Lowered twelve feet down into a grave of solid rock,
So anxious was he to deny all doctors taking stock;
And yet in spite of all of this he too was disinterred -
Quite the most disgraceful thing that I have ever heard.

Ireland was a place well-known for giants in olden time.
St. Patrick excavated a twelve-footer in his prime.
Another of this size was excavated from a bog.
When found he was as fossilised as if he were a log.
To prove my point that all good giants end up in England fair,
This one was no exception - and was examined there,
At Broad Street Station, coffined up, in Eighteen Seventy-Six,
His ownership disputed, like some old box of tricks.

Eighteen Sixty-Five brought charming Frenchman Joseph Brice,
Polite and affable, 'good-natured' - frankly rather nice.
Eight feet he was in height and with the public all the rage
As 'Anak - Giant of Giants' - his rôle upon the London stage.
He found not only fame but comfort of an English wife,
As close a couple as you'd find in this old world of strife.

Giants from North America liked London - then, as now,
The Showbiz capital of all the world, you will allow.
Captain Martin Bates, and Ann his wife, both came from there,
Each being nearly eight feet tall, as many now declare.
'Exhibited' in London, in Eighteen Seventy-One,
They married at St. Martin-in-the-Fields, figures of fun.

The tallest Englishman the young John Middleton was he,
Who lived from Fifteen Seventy-Eight to Sixteen Twenty-Three.
Known as The Childe of Hale, to nine feet three some say he grew,
Though this is now disputed, so no-one really knew.

One of several engravings by H. Carpenter showing
Cuckfield's giant Henry Blacker, whose admirers among
English society of the 1750s included King George III.

Pound for pound our very own man Daniel Lambert's hard to match,
In Eighteen Hundred Six weighed fifty stones. From floor to thatch
A John Bull archetype and celebrated oddity,
He dwelt in Piccadilly, at number Thirty-Three,
And there was visited by all the fashionable set,
As nice a chap, they say, as you could ever hope to get.

Joachim Eleizegue, a Spaniard, came to Dover
When he had grown some seven feet eight, and maybe slightly over.
The Cosmorama, Regent Street, is where they would announce it -
But such a name! No Londoner quite managed to pronounce it.

Eighteen Eighty brought to town Norwegian giant Von Brusted
To London stage where he was 'shown' and also widely toasted.
In Nineteen Five, *at nine feet three(?)* appeared at the Palladium
The Russian Machnow - Giants *that* size could fill the Wembley
                                                                    Stadium!

For giants of any age and size it was a lonely life
And very hard for many of the men to find a wife.
Hist'ry proves, however, female giants, though rare, are found,
Though to meet with satisfaction one's obliged to cover ground.
Across three centuries came lots of foreign giantesses,
Over seven feet, from varnished toe-nail to their tresses.
Pepys in Holborn saw a Nederlander giantess,
In fact he took his wife, so failed to get the girl's address.
That was in the Sixteen Sixties. Lady giants came many
To Fleet Street taverns where you'd not expected to see any.

A state called 'daddy-long-legs syndrome' sadly affects some.
Bernard Coyne of Iowa one such fellow to succumb.
Eight feet two at time of death, his growing still unchecked,
In World War One the Army had no option but reject -
Another of those fellows illness grants in years no more
Than twenty-two or twenty-three. He died at twenty-four.
Many such conditions have proved far from heaven-sent.
No-one can say, as oft today, 'twas the *environment.*

The biggest man recorded in the files of medicine
Was Robert Pershing Wadlow, one of Illinois' men.

His growth accelerated after infant surgery
For a bilateral hernia. It was the same for me:
For that same state much later *I* was operated on
At - mark you - fifty-five and so less sorry it was done.
Less than one inch short of nine feet tall poor Wadlow grew,
Then died in Nineteen Forty, aged only twenty-two.

One can't escape conclusion that the giants of the past
Were much maligned and kinder than the rôle in which they're cast.
Even modern giants, though sociable, lived in mortal fear
Of medicine and science and museums, it is clear,
For so many of the surgeons then deemed respectable
Were avid for large skeletons, appendages and all.
Therefore, let's mount a Festival, demanding wide compliance,
To pay for past abuses, inhumanity to giants,
Obliterating images of circus side-show freak
And of giant tenderness and giant dignity let's speak.

Today, we overpopulate
The planet, so statistics state,
And millions more than we have guessed
Pollute the earth, which we infest.
On facts you may not place reliance,
Yet we now find fewer giants
(Though we may not yet have traced all
Seven-footers playing baseball
Or who throw balls in high baskets
Taller than which sport no task gets).

Think what fun 'twould be if we
Encountered one, say eight-feet-three,
Coming out of King's Cross Station.
Wouldn't that confound the nation?

As for all that's past repair,
Respect and awe should come to bear,
For now and then in giant mound
A giant's skeleton is found.
Disturb you not a single bone.

To earn good luck leave well alone,
For giants' lives were of short lease,
Therefore deserve being left in peace.

William Evans, the King's Porter, and Jeffrey
Hudson the Dwarf.
From a stone relief that once stood in Bullhead Court, Newgate
Street, in the City of London.

Good Tempered Giants *has been offered to BBC Radio Four as a
narration 'for two voices', which it is; but the main reason for
constructing it in such varying, long and short metre was to avoid what
I call the* Hiawatha *effect!*

I enjoy teasing eggheads and have not even spared the blushes of Professor Stephen Hawking of the Department of Experimental Physics, Cambridge, who from time to time reflects illustriously on the subject of the Universe.

I appreciate that, due to his disability, he is unable to reply to correspondence; but he is not without a sense of humour, so in March 1995 I wrote to him saying I was putting together another volume of verse similar to Poetry on Purpose, *a copy of which I enclosed. I said it had long been a contention of mine that the universe (indeed, the entire multiplicity of universes) has a corporate 'life' of its own, but that we are all too dumb (or too small) to recognise it. I tempted him to respond to the following piece of doggerel - just for a bit of fun.*

His secretary replied with crushing brevity that he could not supply a quote for Poetry on Purpose. *This was not, of course, what I'd asked for.* Poetry on Purpose *was already published, as was self-evident.*

I accepted the rebut philosophically, but very nearly wrote back to say 'no wonder the secrets of the universe remain a secret!'

THE COD-ROE MULTIVERSE

Astronomers and physicists - and worse! -
   Have odd ideas about the universe.
Their cobbled theories are far from done,
   Though ready now t'admit there's more than one -

More than one universe, that is to say:
   But I've known this for fact for many a day
And could have told them so and set them free
   From reams of algebra and chemistry.

Each universe is like a single ovum,
   Alongside countless others, where God stove 'em
Into a sort of multiversal *roe*
   Of infinite size. Each egg is left to grow.

But each of them is very far from bland
   And each (to one inside) seems to expand,
Which is just what an ovum's s'posed to do
   Until a thing quite wonderful breaks through:

For all at once, from all these milt elations,
   A trillion multifish configurations
Explode into a trillion multi-fish -
   More universes than a chap could wish.

b

Ordin'ry fellers reas'nably suppose
   A scientist can see beyond his nose;
But eggheads think this notion's overblown:
   A Universe with life to call its own!

TELECOMMUNICATIONS

When Gaea to humankind permitted birth,
   The biggest man-made artefact on earth
Was a direct result. With much remorse,
   I say it grew from craving intercourse.
I speak of the communications mesh
   That girdles Earth from Perth to Marrakesh.

From this inevitable consequence
   There grew a competition quite intense
For phone and fax and radio emission,
   Telemetry and cabled television.
What's more, the sky itself was full of kites
   They called communications satellites.

The planet now has a distinctive throb
   Resembling kettle boiling on a hob.
Was this upgraded universal part
   Desired by Gaea from the very start?
All seemed to grow from human much ado,
   But one should ask oneself: *who's using who?*

CLEAN DECK IN A FLICK CARTOON

A curious new Theory of Time
I here incorrigibly express in rhyme,
For while I'm sure it isn't without fault,
I set it down as something of this sort:

It's not a process flowing always past.
Each moment is distinguished from the last,
Frozen like snapshots, or a pack of cards,
Each like a frame seen when a film retards.

Does each of these within its own time-slot
Slip into dull oblivion? It does not!
Each frame, each snapshot, stays within existence,
Continuing in life with much persistence.

Time-travellers intrepid thus could find
Each incident, each action, left behind
In stroboscopic trail, preserved, not lost,
But letters in a universal post,

Which in unbroken sequence one could get
Like cards out of a filing cabinet:
Each moment photographed, freeze-framed - forever
Recoverable (be it with some endeavour).

It follows, then, why some religions should
Be so insistent that we all be good.
They do not wish Time's river to pollute
With naughty deeds, but Virtue Absolute.

Next time you're tempted, bear in mind this thought:
Your sins live on where acts of goodness ought.

STAR GRAZING

I've just come back
From spearing stars -
And so I nothing lack.
From the springboard of Mars
Got high on
Orion.
Looked for a pretty nurse
On Betelgeuse.
Swam in the pan
Of the Great Bear.
Got a nice tan.
Found healing everywhere
And now that I've been,
Feel clean.

COMMUNICATION

Knowing the universe is so immense
May mean that God's regard is less intense,
That we're not quite as Chosen as we'd wish.
Do you think it safe to assume God speaks English?

I wrote 'Modern Dimes' in May 1995, shortly after our nation had cele-brated the 50th Anniversary of Victory in Europe. An ardent patriot, I joined in that celebration wholeheartedly; but in the back of my mind were several recent examples of what I call the warfare of economics. You have only to recall the sterling crisis in 1992 when dark forces behind international currency speculation forced Britain's withdrawal from the European Exchange Rate Mechanism.

Mischievously, I posted a draft of the poem to Dr Hans Tietmeyer of the Deutsche-Bundesbank in Frankfurt, asking if he agreed modern banks are as Machiavellian as I implied. 'Enter into the spirit of the thing', I wrote, 'and suggest a suitable title. "Modern Dimes" is just a pun on "Modern Times".'

There are those who say Germans have no sense of humour. At any rate, Herr Tietmeyer did not reply. But people who don't answer my letters do so at their peril. Something I learned from working many years in broadcast-ing is that when an invitation to be interviewed is declined, the newscaster always says so, leaving behind just the faintest suggestion of guilt . . .

MODERN DIMES

No one need anymore engage in war,
As they have done so many times before.
Forget the armoury, the planes, the tanks,
The bombs, the soldiery of many ranks.

All you need do, a nation to destroy,
Is plan a cunning economic ploy:
Just undermine your enemy - perhaps
By causing his exchange rate to collapse

And buying while the rate is very low,
Ensuring currency's no place to go
Except into your own bank's hungry vault,
Reducing thus your enemy to nought.

Better far, by subtle speculation,
Employing an almighty computation,
To starve a nation of its very bread
Than have the rivers, oceans, running red.

Your foe in economic subjugation,
You may enjoy a national celebration.
The only cost for sounding Victory's hooter
Is just a simple sum on your computer.

KILL THE FRONT PAGE . . . NEW HEADLINE!

God said, rise now:
I have things for you to do today
And things for you to say
And things from which you may not turn away.
No time now for delay.
This is the hour for holding men at bay.
Too late now to allay
Their fears. It's time to pay
The price for having not done what they may,
For having repeatedly responded Nay
To my Commandments. I'll no longer stay
My hand, no longer listen while they bray.

The time has come for different ways to pray, for
        MAN IS NOT FIRST!
        MAN IS THE *WORST!*
He may no longer this fair earth besmirch.
Time for a new *Environmental* Church!
And Man his head to bow.
Come, I will show you how.

I wrote the following lyric in the hope that, one day, I'd have the pleasure of meeting Elton John and that he'd agree to set it to music. If he is out there and listening, may I remind him that 'hope too long deferred maketh the heart sick' . . . ?

BEDTIME STORY

We are Octopus,
Exuding ink, ink, ink.
Hard to find us
In the drink, drink, drink.

Hi-tail inland
For a mile
And you'll find us,
Crocodile,
On the dank, dank, dank
River bank.

How our teeth ground
As they sank !

We are Dinosaur,
Up on the tor, tor, tor;
You'll also find us
On the valley floor.
Please don't trouble
The woods to comb,
We will visit
You at home.
On reflection,
Should you care,
We're already,
Already there.

DEADHEAD THE DAFFODILS

Be swift
In search of crocuses
And let them lie;
But deadhead the daffodils
When they die.
Leave the leaves whole
To slow decay,
Investing goodness
For another day.

Leave every bulb
Quite undisturbed.
In doing so,
Be not perturbed,
For all the richness
Of the leaf
Will die back slow -
No call for grief.

Drawn down into
Its onion womb,
Each pregnant bulb
Will grow for you
Another bloom
And pleasure bring
Again come early spring.

SUMMER AT KEW

Kew Gardens - that's my kind of place;
    But *visitors* - they're a disgrace.
Out comes the sun: the Joans and Sids
    Arrive with swarms of rampant kids.

They haven't come to see the plants,
    They've come to rant and rage and prance.
No use complaining, for you find
    Both Mum and Dad are deaf and blind.

I stand confounded and aloof,
    For nothing there is infant-proof.
I long for gardeners to breed
    An infant-eating plant from seed.

Kew Gardens - that's my kind of place,
But - God! - I hate the human race.

FOR GOD'S SAKE, NOAH, WHERE ARE YOU?

An unticketed tourist, you,
Here on a visit
To
God's zoo.

Life in here is simply dire
Since the global forest fire.
All the keepers have departed
(They were among the first that started).
It is bedlam now entire.
What a terrible ado!

Only if you are a lark
Are you welcome on God's Ark,
For the waters now are rising on the land.
Tea and buns will not go round,
We shall sink or run aground,
Though we continue such a merry band.

Persist and climb aboard:
You will find a dwindling hoard
And the flood is now high up above my knee.
If only we had planned
To have a Skipper in command . . .

Doves of peace are flying over empty sea.

GREENING

Forgive, Lord, one who cometh a long league
And finds within less charity than charity-fatigue,
Less love for Man, of pity for him dearth,
But much compassion for the starveling Earth.

During 1993-4 I was an occasional visitor to St. Ives, in Cornwall, which involved catching the Penzance train from London-Paddington. Following this familiar route on Christmas Eve, 1994, proved something of a disappointment. It involved a very early start on a bitterly cold day, discovering the heating on the train had failed and that the only available buffet service had run out of breakfast trays when only just clear of London. The return journey was, if anything, even worse, but the railmen apologised handsomely.

WESTWARD BOUND

Dawn breaks through an ice-blue sky
On frosted land, as far as eye
Can see, for 'spite befuddled brain,
I managed just to catch the train
And though I'm only half alive
On the Seven Twenty-Five
From Paddington, t'ward town and tide,
Cold and breakfastless I ride,
In a kind of waking trance -
A long way yet before Penzance.

CHANGE AT ST. ERTH
(In Praise of St. Ives)

On hippety-hoppity train
I'm coming back to quaint St. Ives again,
To drawn-with-a-ruler horizon,
To never-drawn-bluer horizon,
Which sun and sea bedizen,
Where gulls dip, screech and splatter
And then cry '*What's the matter . . . ?*'

Ever seen Carbis Bay
In the full flood of day?
Ever had
Sight of such pretty girl and comely lad?
Have you set eyes on
Cobbled streets that turn so meetly,
Where baskets hang so sweetly,
Either with fish or flower?
Take your pick and choose your hour.
St. Ives is an artist's palette.
Dip your brush, or bring your mallet
To free the rocks of purple amethyst.
O, let me twist
Your arm. Such pleasant bars!
(You'll have to dodge the dogs and motor-cars.)

Nowhere in England are you so well fed,
Or find so big and comfortable a bed.
Begone, dull City dives!
Pray, do not lag -
Quick, pack a bag
And join me in St. Ives.

WHALE ON THE BEACH

It lay there on the sand,
Steered by an unseen hand
To journey's end,
No longer able to defend
Itself, there on the beach,
Exposed, yet somehow strangely out of reach,
For never one had it been wont to find
Of its own kind,
But felt itself quite desolately lone,
Its days all done.

Wistful guardian angels stood around
Where it had run aground.
They prayed and kept it moist,
Rolled upright, kept it hoist
In shallows where it whimpered, craving rest,
Yet it did not protest.

It once had found itself alive
Where Nature's epicentre did contrive
A simple natural Law for all Creation
And it had known sensation,
Had once the power to wonder,
When it rose, leapt, then alternately dived under
Bracing waters - or so one might suppose;

But now it was alone.
Its watery wonderland had turned to stone,
The pain
Too strong for one to want to long remain.

And though the angels struggled to revive
A thing so marvellous, meant to be alive,
All it wanted was to sleep,
Had no longer the desire or will to keep
The unavailing struggle to survive,
Desired to die,
For even stars grow weary of the sky.

Strong, strong may be a whale's divine belief,
But then at last there came to it relief
So sudden, there was barely time to pray,
So soon night followed day:

A vet with single hypodermic thrust
Put end to all he really thought he must.

At once, the whale's soul
Fell through a giant black hole
And somewhere else was seen,
As if its recent past had never been.

The earth it left
Was bereft.
Angels that had fought so hard to save it,
Hardly forgave it,
Watering the sand with unconsoling tears
They would remember their surviving years.

There remained,
Sun-bright and sparklingly sustained,
The wide ocean - far as one could see . . .
That whale - it was a metaphor for me.

BREAKFAST AT FIGARO'S

Good morning, sir!
Cómo está usted?
English breakfast? Certainly.
Bacon? Egg? Sausage? Tomato? Mushroom?
                          Chips? Beans? Fried bread?

With toast, please.
Toast I'd like best
And everything well done . . .

Coffee, sir? Juice?

. . . But do the eggs a trifle loose.

Trifle, sir? Certainly.

Er . . . I think not.

Sit down, sir. Take your coffee.
We bring your breakfast to you nice and hot.

A FRANCOPHOBE IN PARIS

We drank champagne, ate Quiche Lorraine,
Despite my Francophobe disdain.
We fought the two World Wars again.

Our hotel? Near the Gare somewhere:
I saw my first nude woman there,
But found a cockroach on the stair;
In bed, a tell-tale stain.

We went to bistros where a toff'll
Eat most awful kinds of offal -
Dishes poshly named, that gain
For Englishmen much stomach pain.

The Paris stage for nudity
Was unsurpassed in lewdity;
The songs (of mostly blue ditty)
Were largely ones of crudity.

City of incongruities,
Demanding large gratuities,
Paris may stay just where it is:
I say it plain.

THE AMERICAN TOURIST

Americans were there.
Their conversation was inclined to blare,
Strident and strong
With nasal twang
And chewing-gum diphthong.
Their voices rang,
Striking like gong:
One sang a patter-song,
Brash
As corned beef hash,
Or Kong
Made up in a sarong.
Such confidence inflates
Those who come from the United States! -
Confident of what's right
(Viewed from the dollar's might),
But sometimes wrong.

One, for a dare,
Asked me the way to Piccadilly *Square*.
I said it was a Circus,
Then thought how it would irk us
To improvise a Big Top
(Somewhere near the bus-stop?)
Just to please them there,
With clowns and tamers, acrobats and horses,
Bounding round the courses
Of poor old Eros with his silent stare.

THE WINE-SHIPPER'S PRICE LIST

A casual claret? Pray do not abstain.
The '61 Mouton-Rothschild once again?
Its grape sits well with grain.
Or there's Lynch-Bages, including Jereboam,
A humbler range to go with *le fromage*
(Happen to know 'em?).

I note, discreet among the White Bordeaux -
It's little short of heaven,
Don't you know -
A Chateau D'Yquem from Nineteen Sixty-Seven.

Had I a mistress, instead of furs,
Perhaps the sole remainder should be hers
Of Chambolle-Musigny *'Les Amoureuses'* . . .
(Red Burgundy? It says so on the list.
I'll take your word for it, if you insist.)

I will not spurn the
Eighteen Ninety-Three
Dom de Coulom Signonac.
What? All for me?
No - send it back.
In my domain, brandy's just for cooking
(Or sip when no one's looking)!

Instead, for friends who swear much by Madeira,
Gentle the Nineteen Eleven Bual Blandy
A trifle nearer.
Fine and dandy!
One case and three loose bottles left - God wot,
Had I my cheque-book I would take the lot.

AT THE BATHS

Lately I've become quite partial
   To the Epigrams of Martial
And the poems of Catullus
   Which were hardly meant to lull us;

Also possibly for me
   Is The Greek Anthology.
But what need I of classic fads
   At the steam-bath with the lads?

It's hoped we'll all meet, by and by,
   In the Great Steam Bath in the Sky;
Meantime, if the Devil should cast his net,
   My, what a motley haul he'd get!

POETS' POSE

How many odes, I wonder, must I write
before I'm quite
Entitled to the broad-brimmed, floppy hat,
Flowing cravat
And look of dusty, fusty, faded blue
Which comes from too much sun,
An outdoor garden-dun,
Things far from new,
From being in a literary rut,
With no haircut,
A *distant* look
Which comes from poring over many a book,
Then raising eyes on
Some far, lost, unachievable horizon,
Thinking too much
And being just a trifle out of touch?

Tell me, please do.

The above lines were written after seeing an old photograph of the late author and poet Robert Graves, taken when he was well advanced in years; whereupon an unkind coincidence interposed. Only a few weeks later, a dermatologist advised me, with a certain emphasis, to avoid exposure to the sun, recommending among other things some appropriate headgear - so the expectation of a 'broad-brimmed, floppy hat', which I had associated with poets in the elder statesmen class, came upon me somewhat sooner than envisaged.

Poetic justice, perhaps! Fate never intended me for the sunny side of the street.

46

MODERN POETS

They sprinkle words on paper
As if from a pepper-pot
And hardly care
If anyone there
Perceives the sense
              Or not.

Their verses have no cadence;
They do not scan or rhyme,
For which they make no recompense,
But fudge it every time.

They take a stance on assonance
But offer a cruder sound
And many a line that's asinine
They hope will be found profound.

Can it be they'll come to see
Words are not simply toys?
And will that serve to separate
The poets from the boys?

HURTING A POET

Hurting a Poet
Is (you should know it!)
Like injuring one holy:
There's nothing so lowly -
The eighth deadly sin.

What terrible trouble that culprit is in,
For such sin knows barely an expiation
And heaven accepts no explanation.
If you have hurt someone who rhymes,
You'll be reborn a thousand times . . .

First as a cockroach,
Then as a fly,
Then as a serpent
Live and then die.

Repentance is useless,
Forgiveness denied;
You'll live in great torment,
No mercy applied.

Faced with an endless
Succession of births,
One following t'other,
The next will seem worst.
Sting-ier, slimier each than the last
So that you will long for the one that's just past;

And despite your aversion
You'll often experience horrid reversion,
Beginning again from a miserable start
A life quite apart.

Sometimes you'll revert
To amoeba, a-spurt
With division of outlawed, unspeakable cells
Giving off the most acrid, disgusting of smells.

Your hope for improvement on Darwinist ladder
Will result in each effort each time seeming badder.

Till if, at the end,
With conscience amend,
And spirit full-grown
In pride of your own,

If you dare once again
To repeat the offence,
You'll die in dire pain
And begone from here hence.

---

c

KATHLEEN

Might
It seem cheap,
A little trite
And far-fetched, to say
In this way
(For the thought of you makes me weep
And I am not at my best today),
That your voice seems to come to me
From the deep
And deep between
Stars of eternity?
For then I think what might have been.

Eternity was the last word
I heard
You sing in *Das Lied von der Erde*.

When you made
That supremely high-grade
Celebrated recording
(Bruno Walter conducting),
You knew
That you
Were going to
Die,
As you did the year following.

Now
As you sing your Goodbye
(And I keep asking *How?*)
That eternal voice soaring
Surely comes from the sky.

My cousin, Pat Groves, has one of the most comprehensive private collections of recorded music I know of, and it is to him that I owe most of the music I possess. A great influence on my musical appreciation, I include the following for his amusement.

GERMANIC WAGNER

I have been known (and more than once or twice)
To say of Wagner something fairly nice;
Then honesty takes hold and truth takes wing:
I would not like to sit right through *The Ring*.

Far worse than for a manager to bring it
Is for a singer who's obliged to sing it.
No one composer
Is so much like a German-built bulldozer,
For nothing tender
Emerges when old Wagner's on a bender.

Thanks to my cousin,
I have the odd dozen
Wagnerian works in the house.
I much prefer Mahler
Let loose in my parlour,
For the only Wagnerian music I like is by Strauss!

THE ANGELS OF NORWICH

At stage
Of what is sometimes kindly called Third Age,
From London Town I came,
Hoping to find
Something of different kind,
Less of the same
And yet not polyglot,
In search of quiet,
A change of diet.

(I'd passed through grimmest Diss.
Diss I'd not miss a lot!)
A trifle lost,
Commotion-toss'd,
Not to say remiss,
For, without intention
(I'd heard of it no mention),
To your Concert I came late:
The singing did not wait.

Slipping from hot June
Into the cool lagoon
Of cloistered calm,
I was at once wing'd up
Into the balm
Of lovely lierne vaulting.
Wings of angels somersaulting
Came to mind.
No stone is carved so kind.

Music refined
Came from the Choir of Downing,
Robed in mete gowning.

I missed the Brahms
And Walton,
Various psalms,

But not the *Missa O Quam Gloriosum
Regnum est,*
Sung at its best.
This is how angels sing -
No-one accompanying.
Last, far from least,
Zadok the Priest.

O happy congregation
To have such feasts for your sustained elation.
What other company in this glad nation,
Knowing few losses,
Has full Eleven Hundred kindly bosses
Glancing benignly down, 'mid shining crosses? -
In England grand,
The finest such Cathedral in the land.

Look at the nave
And aisles,
So quiet and grave,
The graven tiles,
The lovely groining,
Chapels adjoining,
And the delightful choir!
Of these, who'd ever tire?

In the transept
I sat, transfixed, and wept
For all I saw around,
So sweetly kept
From spire to ground.
No sign of vandals!
I lit two candles,
Placed on arboreal shelf.
(One was, I fancy, for myself.)

Then, feeling at once replete
And finding strength,
Returned at length
Into the unkind heat.

Although I have been a Friend of St. Paul's Cathedral for several years, it was not until July 12th 1995 that I stirred myself to attend the annual Festival of Friends. This event takes place in the Cathedral itself, invariably attended by our Patron, Her Majesty Queen Elizabeth, the Queen Mother. Even so, it was a much grander occasion than I had anticipated. I was struck by the graciousness of our Royal Patron, now well advanced into her 90s, and by the superb quality of the St. Paul's Cathedral Choir, which I have, of course, heard on many similar occasions before.

The Reception which followed took place in the Cathedral Crypt which is where Admiral Lord Nelson and many other great English heroes have their resting place. It was also here that I at last was able to put face to name of our hard-working Secretary to the Friends Robin Sherlock. Write something for us, *he commanded. So I did.*

THE FESTIVAL OF FRIENDS

If, like me,
You're growing sadly short of Family,
Could you do better than, with Friends around,
Where festive trappings everywhere abound,
Be seated here, our glorious Dome above,
With Someone Royal we all uniquely love?
Ladies in summer hats,
Men in cravats,
Where all by choice
Are in good voice
And share a common sense
Of friendship, worship, fellowship intense?
Bells ringing,
Hearts singing,
A hint of mystery,
Pride in our history,
The loyal Bidding . . .

Such fine Anthems,
Done without tantrums!
Those Scamps Galore
Are of the kind you'd hear at heaven's door,
For be you Clerk or Forester
You'll nowhere find a finer chorister
Than within walls
Of Great St. Paul's.

You might the world traverse and fail to hire
A finer Choir.
Purcell and Mendelssohn - and later more.

Farewell at length to our good Patron,
Our gracious Matron.
Would that she'd stayed
And followed to the end our Friends' parade.
For what's more swell, son,
Than sharing a glass with Horatio Nelson?
Few so privileged have sipp'd
Wine in the Crypt.
(Here, too, one might touch forelock
with Robin Sherlock!)

Went home with things bought largely on the hop
In the Gift Shop.
Head ringing,
Heart singing,
Where in good spirit to St. Paul's had been
Our family of Friends so welcome seen.

DEVOTIONS

How many of you in this congregation
Are truly wrapt in concentrated prayer,
Excogitate, not going through the motion?
Can you stand there and in all conscience swear?

Yes, you can make the vaulting ring
When you sing;
But you could sound as often glad (or sorry)
If you were singing (spare us!) *Annie Laurie*.

Fishing from the book of common form,
Are you sincere - or trying to keep warm?
Are you, in your finest Sunday coat,
Quoting by rote?

(There's one who's suffering from painful gout.
To him I give the benefit of doubt.
Like him, I do not feel
At all in shape to kneel.)

Does God still hear us better when and whether
Just two or more are gathered here together?

APOCALYPTIC CULTS

Apocalyptic cults
Are springing up and getting swift results,
Wallowing
In large following,
And, mantled in the strangest of new frocks,
They rant their creeds, recycled and detergent,
While filling many urgent
Variations of the old collection box,

Seizing the hour
To earn not just great wealth but burgeoned power
Over soft-gullible hordes of lads and lasses
From the bewildered masses,
Claiming grave station
Over their thrilling, spilling congregation.

THE GARDEN AT GETHSEMANE

The greatest trial
Is when your God does not appear
To be near
And all the while,
In cloistered agony, tormented pain,
Such birds as sing, unseen, sing all in vain.
Meantime your friends and kith and kindred sleep,
While you weep,
And all you have for company is thorn,
For it's not yet dawn
And you know what anguish waits upon the morn
And you pray
The Cup may be removed from you today,
So, at last,
All suffering is past
And, bless'd to live as others of your age,
You're left to slip quite quietly off the page.

In January 1995, I wrote to Canon John Oates, Rector of St. Bride's, the charming Wren church in London's Fleet Street, long recognised as 'the journalists' church'. I said I had for some time been dismayed at the turn English journalism had been taking, by which I implied that it is more and more inclined toward sensationalism, intrusion into privacy and the exercise of power without responsibility. The words of the following Hymn had sprung to mind. I offered it, thinking it might serve a purpose when a journalistic congregation is in attendance. He wrote back to say that it is true the press act irresponsibly from time to time, but that he saw enough of their work 'and the sacrifices made in the interest of getting news to the public to know that there is another side to the picture.' He did not exactly reject the hymn, reprinted below, but sent me in return a prayer of his own that he uses on press occasions. It was a good one and made me realise I had been presumptuous.

HYMN FOR ST. BRIDE'S

Almighty God, the words with which I deal
    Have both the power to hurt and power to heal.
Grant that I am through Thine insistence proved
    And, by the arrows of the spirit moved,
Reflect Thy will, so that I turn my skill
    To everlasting good and not to ill.

Turn vanity and false ambition, pride
    And other undesired traits aside,
Remembering the gift I have was free
    And given, Lord, unstintingly, by Thee,
Therefore, a skill that was divinely bless'd
    It follows must be subject to Thy test.

Since stipend I am paid for what is Thine,
    Let all my purposes with right combine.
Thy power invested, tempered with justice be
    And Thine own greatness championed by me,
So that I sing Thy glory and Thy praise,
    Integral in the labour of my days.

CHURCH GREEN

You! You're an experienced self-regarder. Search!
Find an excuse for humans, if you can:
We are the only living things on earth
Wilfully sullying in our own life-span
Land, air and ocean - all the things we're taught
That offer life essential life-support.

Help me, therefore, to found a brand-new Church
That title gives to Earth and not to Man.

THE DIVINE SUBCONSCIOUS

The brain of God, it seems,
Is full of troubled dreams.

One day, our kind
Will bubble to the surface of His mind

And thereby find release.
God will at last sleep easy
And His troubles cease.

THE PLAYING FIELDS OF ENGLAND

Of blood and courage are these fields well-laid
    For games that turn upon Dame Fortune's blade;
Therefore rejoice, be proud who came, who dared,
    The poetry of men in glory shared.

EMULATING DARREN GOUGH

I'd like to write a poem of fire and coals,
    Rather as Darren Gough both bats and bowls.
The problem's one of age and turn of line:
    He's a fit twenty; I'm a fat sixty-nine.

FICKLE FANS

Unhappy day
When motley, lumpen, lumbering
Louts appeared outnumbering,
A jealous, fickle mob
Who love to rob
A master of his glory,
And so debunk his story,
Who nothing do but bay
At the rare gifted
And, though ten thousand times before uplifted,
Turned on its one-time hero
As he plumped to zero
And, one and all,
Gloried in his downfall.

It was a great, great day
For those whose joy it is to sneer
And snipe and jeer
And scoff and goad and boo,
When *Ooh, ah, Cantona*
Turned into crude *Yah-hoo!*

POOR HUGH!

Is it his fault,
Or more the way we're taught?

Were we less sentimental
And not quite so judgemental,
Society less prude
In moral attitude,
Getting hard
On Sunset Boulevard
Would just be thought
A trifle rude.

The victim might with justice guilt refute:
It was the street supplied the prostitute.

HAZARDS

If it's true that Life is a White-Knuckle Ride on a Roller-Coaster,
It is best, I attest, if you share a place in its Twin-Slice Toaster;
It's much less fun as you leap on the run in the Mincer-Grinder,
But to share each shove with one that you love will be kinder.

SIN-CHRONOUS LOVE

You know those sequential Russian dolls
That fit one within one within another?
And those Chinese boxes,
Carved with a lovetime's patience,
One within one within another?

You must be familiar
With ardour like that,
When you fall irretrievably and irredeemably in love with
                                    someone
Though already inextricably, ineluctably
In love with someone else.

Some believe that cannot happen,
That such inconstancy
Betrays a fickle nature.
Wrong.
You dote on both,
One as much as t'other, in your way,
Just differently,
In varying degree.
A weathercock, I'm sure someone would say:
Passion ought not t'exceed
A proper ration or a decent need.

I will go further.
'Tis not unknown
For fiery natures such as - well - your own,
Burdened with such ineffable desire
And so on fire
As to love *many* more than most require.
More than just two
At once, that is.
Sorry - you sometimes do.

I do not say
Such love's returned in every single way
Out of respect for one so often burned
(In fact, sometimes it's positively spurned);
But then, to be so bountifully in thrall's
A gift that is not given to us all.
What said Saint Paul -
Marry or burn?
Well, you will never learn.

You are incurably imbued
With amorous amplitude,
With replicate attitude,
Quite like those Russian dolls,
With painted polls,
Or like a Chinese box,
Designed to tease and puzzle and to fox,
Carved with the patience of a mother,
One within one within another.

———————————————————

MENTOR

I wanted to play Socrates
To your Alcibiades.
You had the looks,
I had the books
And sought to 'shoot the breeze'.

The trouble is you wanted both the rôles,
In consequence of which we're several poles
Apart.

The younger, you'd the better start.
Now you are older
And (like your model) bolder:
You still snap off erections
From the sacred sections
Of hallowed herms
(In metaphoric terms).

Once, when by chance you met me,
You hurled a slipper at me
Because I plain refused
To sup with you when you were rather boozed.

You stood for my high dudgeons,
I, your defaced escutcheons,
And there is peace between us,
A kind of kindness, nothing heinous.
Deceitful you were not:
What one saw was what one got.

Now I - still prone to cock
A sidelong snoot - sip slow the grim hemlock.
But Oh, I do implore you,
Though legions still adore you,
No longer seek
To emulate the Greek.
Let your ways mend
Lest like young Kibbie come to sticky end.

A MAN REMEMBERED
(for R.M.)

We found in you
A diamond, to whose hue
No craftsman would have sought to add a shine,
But thought you fine,
For not a movement
Required any polish or improvement;
A man of sinew,
With not an ounce of harm or malice in you.
A man of fibre.
A good imbiber!
And, in your prime,
A man for any tide and any time.

You were the only man a man could kiss
And not be thought amiss;
And you were strong
In ways wherein most other men are wrong.
And I recall, in memory long since hid,
A thing requiring greatness that you did,
Out of your strength of heart and mind and limb,
A loyalty that never waxes dim;
And many other deeds at life's frayed hem
That left us richer for the knowing them.

Now, despite the many seasons taught them,
Comes each man's autumn
And every leaf, once green,
Rich russet falls, though there have many been.
Yet in our hearts your summer is still whole:
A man remembered in a model rôle.

VISION OF THE ABYSS

One night, I fear, with soul all unredeemed,
Your life will slip into a dream I've dreamed,
Where, basketed like cold, left-over chips,
Lie fag-ends of all past relationships.

And God will lock the door of your escape,
Leaving no ward, where devils prod and jape
On murky pavements, and the dark connects
With trash no garbage-man ever collects.

There, chained and straining in the dream's backyard,
A lurid devil in a leotard,
And bunched like dull, black, bitter, unpicked grapes,
Some sins unborn in strangely spectral shapes:

While stagnant gutters mercilessly drip
A taint that's noisome to the urgent sip;
Where scattered hopes, stamped with the night's assay,
Lie dank in cells unwindowed to the day.

Sad friends and family will never know,
Thinking you dead, your spirit still in tow,
Coffined alive within the unseen black,
Appealing help . . . but never coming back.

CURTHOSE GIANTS

Often, my heroes
Are scrum-halves.
Neither milk-sops
Or tight-head props,
But ones who, qualifying as my *braves*,
Being short in height must needs to be on their toes.

I speak of the likes
Of Nelson, Mahler, Lawrence and Lautrec:
Men who 'got on their bikes'
While bigger ones stayed stagnant below deck.

The short-arse man who dares to compensate
I find I rarely hate,
Especially if he's one who's fought
And won;
In short,
My son,
Some men are great though physically small;
Stature's a thing that matters not at all.

In 1994, my friend John Davies, knowing of my interest in our national hero, Lawrence of Arabia, sent me a cutting from the magazine Motor Cycle *containing a touching reference to the great man. The motor-cycle fraternity respected Lawrence as an authority on, and owner of, the celebrated Brough Superior - a model he rode for many years, but on which, in 1935, he had his fatal accident. The item reported that, although every year since his death someone had met the cost of placing a floral tribute on his grave, the arrangement had for the first time been discontinued. This affected me, for I greatly deplored the mood of scepticism and prevailing fashion of destructive self-denigration that informs our national media and reduces our nation and our national heroes below the status they deserve; but it happened, too, that, at the time, I was regularly visiting the grave of my mother, Emily Groves, who died in 1991. In my estimation, she had been something of an unsung civilian heroine of World War II. Somehow, the two images became fused in the following lines, which I wrote in memory of both those disparate, but greatly loved, personalities. Prior to publication, a cherished friend and former colleague, Ian Barr, was the only person to whom I confided them. Sadly, he himself died in May, 1995, and I was pleased to have the poem accepted in his memory also.*

I am happy to add the news that, despite all, flowers still regularly appear on Lawrence's grave.

REMEMBRANCE

My poem is the rose
That I would place, fresh, dewy, on your grave
Each day, were there a way,
Though it is sentimental, I suppose.

I would prefer your face,
Laughing with life that much to others gave,
For, in your hour,
You were as selfless as the fresh-blown flower
And gave us so much more
Than can be answered for
Or set down bare in ordinary prose.

STONY HEART

How can you know how much
It means to me to know
And see and touch
You? For would you, anyhow,
Care
What sorrow and despair
Are felt by one so yearning
For someone else returning
No hint of joy, no flicker of attention
Deserving of a mention?
You for whom I feverishly burn
Find it so easy utterly to spurn,
And think it even dutiful
To frown on what to me
Alone is beautiful,
But can never be.

MARITAL INSANITY

I know a man whose wife is going mad.
His plight
Is just not knowing how he might
Capture the storm in a dragnet-balloon
And then draw tight
The string
So that the thing
Is close confined
And all the flash and thunder of the mind
Gathered into a kind of bouncing moon,
From which the sick brain
Cannot escape again
And resolute, emboldened, soon
Have it at last controlled.

As things stand,
For him there's neither peace nor helping hand,
Since the unbridled wanton rants and raves,
Having forgotten how a wife behaves,
And tries to draw
With cunning disposition
And tireless attrition
Into her maelstrom maw,
Into the chaos of her wild condition,
Her unhappy spouse
And, with him, all the house.

Saddest of all
Is how he manages amid the squall,
Quiet, mild-mannered, amiable and kind,
Patient and tolerant of the troubled mind,
So that I ask: is this a problem faced?
Or is such tenderness a mite misplaced?
How long before their children, and then he,
Become so deep embroiled,
Despite the way they've toiled,
Find no escape from her insanity
And though themselves are sane,
Never find happiness within again?
Therefore, whom durst
I pity first?

d

THE WIND EXCHANGE

It was one of those days
When the wind didn't seem to know
Which of a choice of ways
In which to blow.

And the Government of the time,
Well into its prime,
Seemed unable to learn
From any U-turn,
Being stuck. And determined not to go.

While every politician
In the general unease
Of frantic Opposition
(Being desperately short of ammunition
Or other ways to please
Or bore us),
Searched through Roget's Thesaurus
For provocative words like 'Sleaze'
And so start a hungering
For scandal-mongering.

Whether man's or woman's,
The wind exchanged
In what we call The House of Commons,
Seems half deranged
And nobody seems keen
To comprehend what plainly the signs mean:

There are too many people
Demanding too much,
Chasing few jobs
And Freebies and such,
That frequent birth
Eats too much Earth.
Still, we all carry on
As if heaven-sent,
Breeding away
To our hearts' content.

BUY *BIG ISSUE!*

"Buy-Big-Issue?"
Chants the lad
By Moorgate Station.
A trifle sad,
Yet he says it with elation,
Not like sneeze requiring tissue.

At times, when I am sauntering past,
I ask myself how long he'll last,
Standing there as if on tether,
Braving every kind of weather.

"Buy-Big-Issue!"
What a wheeze
If one pretends it's Japanese.
I go into a Nippon café,
Making out I'm rather daffy,
Rather more than I would wish you -
"Think I'll have some *Buy-Big-Issue!*
Is it raw, like Nippon fish,
Or cooked more like I think I'd wish?"

"Oh, everything we serve here's raw,
Sometimes it's still alive, what's more.
Asparagus, with juicy tips?
It doesn't come with peas and chips . . ."

"Buy-Big-Issue . . ."
Often said
(This feller never drops his head!)
"If you were not there, we'd miss you",
Says a lady, quite well-bred,
"Don't want someone else instead.
Like the ones who sell us poppies,
Smiles are worth a thousand copies.
You deserve to be well-fed! . . . "

IDYLL OF THE COUCH POTATO

They lounge and watch a glamour 'soap',
    One redolent of luxury,
That promises success and hope
    Of sex and sloth and sun and sea.

Chic beach clubs, private Swiss accounts,
    Smart women, handsome swells,
Swish social rounds and champagne founts
    And diamond mines and oil wells.

What do they do to earn remission
    And claim the life thought heaven-sent?
They sit and watch their television
    And moan about the Government!

SCHOOL REPORTS

I found an early school report:
Impressed by my young scholarship,
It seemed to say I was the sort
Who'd make a carpenter one day,
Or possibly a clerk, if taught.

No hint that it might come to pass
That I might rise above my class
And that perhaps in course of time
I'd sit like this inventing rhyme,
Or that (it might be fondly wished)
I'd even get it - well - published.

To the surprise of my relations
I quite exceeded expectations.
Therefore, the burthen of this story
Is - whether Liberal, Lab or Tory -
Perchance, if they read 'out of sorts',
Pray pay no heed to school reports.

DO YOU STILL DANCE?

Well, I never!
Did you ever?
Long time no see!
Will you take tea?
Sugar and cream?
How well you seem!
But what an age it's been!
Something tasty?
A Cornish pasty?
Do you still cruise?
Do tell me your news.
I married again -
The one with the brain.
No, not the honey,
The one with the money.
Oh well, my dear,
One has to think clear
For, after all, passion
Is so out of fashion.
I've done with romance.
Do you still dance?

Remember Helen Fairfax-Howe,
An archetypical poor cow,
True to the image of sad *vache*
Always wore a slight moustache,
So plain, so *so* devoid of huggage,
No-one ever helped with luggage?
Well, my dear, she went *afrique,*
Married a prince in Mozambique;
Covered now with jools and jades
And marches with him in parades.

They tell me Nigel Fosters-Coppice -
Lovely lad who showed such promise -
Might have graced the loftiest hall,
But grew to be full eight feet tall,
Which can be a distressing state

If one is hunting for a mate;
But landed just the job in time,
Playing The Giant in Pantomime.

Cora Lake still entertains,
But only men with lots of brains.
Like Alma Mahler, so it's said,
Takes only genius to bed.

Dame Eloise's squire meant
Not to take early retirement,
But The City's not, you see,
What it was once cracked up to be.
She's got what she's too shy to mention:
Thrice the man on half the pension.

Dashing Curly Marshall, he
Married a girl from Winchelsea,
But his mother's sadly missed:
The wife's a rampant feminist.
Now she herself's a mum-to-be,
She eats for two, he cooks for three.

Henrietta Wilberforce
Is now into her *fourth divorce.*
Being American, when she says it,
Sounds like a loathsome frog, of course.
It's not the random spawning habit,
Or that she's breeding like a rabbit -
For who's to know the rights or wrongs? -
It's just the chewing-gum diphthongs!

One cultivates sobriety
When one is in society,
But Gerry Catchpole-Quentin-Gore
Was found quite helpless on the floor
At White's - not once but twice before -
And though quite firmly shown the door,
Just couldn't stand, so stayed for *more.*
He now lives in remotest Kent,
Cashiered from his *chic* regiment.

Poor Dolly Feinstein came to grief
And wrecked her latest on the reef.
Young, handsome and well-exercised,
He baulked at being circumcised;
But *such* a hunk - how could she dump
A youth with such a lovely rump?

That sweet Bertie Forders,
Who took holy orders,
He landed in jail
(My dear, what a tale!) -
Through some indiscretion
At a choir session.
In the midst of Bach's Cantata
Declared a person quite *non grata.*
And his mother's very vexed.
I heard her cry *Whatever next?*

Remember poor Elsie?
She moved out of Chelsea;
Came down in the world,
Her banner quite furled.
Buys second-hand *Diors,*
Wears horrid cheap gewgaws
From shops out-of-town.
Quite lets the side down.

My hair's such a sight,
My nails are a fright.
My dear, that the *time?*
But it's been *sublime.*
I'll get the bill.
Let's race to the till.
Damn! I've no change.
Can you arrange?
I *am* such a sinner.
You must come to dinner.
Really must fly.
So nice. Bye, bye!

MODS & MADONNAS OF STYLE

Fashion, it seems to me, produces clones.
Men who are better able
Buy for the couture label,
Glad rags
With fancy tags.

Women in gold *lamé*
In the middle of day
Might have more care
For evening wear.

O Jessicas and Jills and Joans and Pams,
A micro-skirt on those appalling hams?
Stop fussing over how to clad your bones.
Women that live in vast blouses shouldn't wear cones.

Duet: Snapshots from London's East End, Circa 1930.

WOMAN OF THE POORER CLASS

A woman of the poorer class,
    Plain to look at, cleaning brass,
Poorly clad and fed, 'twould seem
    And this her Cinderella dream:

A handsome lover on a horse
    Who'd snatch her from this grate, of course,
And take her to some place afar
    To live on love and caviare.

ANNIE COGGINS' WRINGER

All day long, Annie Coggins' wringer
Made its heavy, melancholy sound,
As a ton of other people's washing
Went swishing and sloshing
Through the rollers as she wound
Her mangle,
Wring and untangle, wring and untangle,
Around and around.

Annie Coggins' pinafore was wet
And her shoes sodden,
But her spirit wasn't conquered yet,
Nor her soul leaden.
Annie Coggins had no time to think herself poor;
Annie Coggins' heart was on fire
And burned with desire
For the feller next door.

Trio: Variations on a Theme of Voltaire's

On Meurt deux foix, je le vois bien:
Cesser d'aimer et d'etre aimable,
C'est une mort insupportable.
Cesser de vivre, ce n'est rien
                              - Voltaire (1694-1778)

Not once, but twice we know death's sting:
Ceasing to love, and loved by none,
That's the insufferable one.
Breathing one's last is no great thing.

————————————

We die twice o'er: I see it all so clear.
The end of loving and of being loved -
That's th'intolerable way to be removed
Death of the body's neither there nor here.

————————————

This I see plain: one may die twice:
When neither loved nor loving we
Can know no greater agony.
Ceasing to live is - just not nice.

ESSENCE OF NORFOLK

Sweet bee-hung lavender,
Providing provender
For many a honey tea,
Lilac flower perfume
For many a room,
One way or how
Cooling the fevered brow,
O sacred bloom,
That's so much given
To laid-up linen,
What can you do for me? -
For I do not falter
To splash on your refreshing toilet water.

DISORIENTATION

A stranded bee, laden with pollen,
Dizzy with heat,
Walks uncertain at my uncertain feet,
An archetypal old cross-patch,
Alone, with door left on the latch.
We've things in common,
Each being a disoriented case,
With the odd marble loose, or not in place,
Yet each with just enough inside the coffer
Still to have just a little bit to offer.

SPARROW

Poor wee London sparrow.
Chirping at the conurbated concrete,
Following the straight and narrow,
Ever unremittingly discreet.

O for a peacock's tail,
A parrot's plumage, gaudy,
Never to be sparrow-pale,
But bold and brash and bawdy.

THE SUN WILL SHINE

When there is rain,
Get wet your face
And feel it without pain,
With your Lord's blessing.
Let life come on apace,
Keep future guessing.
The Wheel must turn again.

All is not woe;
Many's the compensation
And though there's far to go,
Many's the station.

And so with every stage
Comes change of stance.
After the storm's cruel rage
The sunbeams dance.

Though fate may not requite,
Hold the reins fast.
Put the Devil to flight:
No pain can last
And though you doubt,
At length all's balanced out.

PARAPLEBEIAN

He's not an Earl, nor yet a Bart.,
He's rather more the young upstart
And such a fussy sort of fart:
How dare it rain on Mr Squart!

GRACE AND GRAIN

Was even Eden free of daily grief?
To think so would most surely stretch belief,
For everything that grows must share in sorrow
And without hurt nought could survive the morrow;
So learn the trick that kicks against the pain
And find sweet passion in the wind and rain.

e

CONVICTION

I speak the truth, Cassandra said,
But nobody believes me.
Thus wrote Aeschylus, long since dead.
His *Oresteia* grieves me:
Cassandra's plight is mine all right -
Frustration's what it leaves me.

BLOOMING ROSES!

As you grow older
And life becomes a big Perhaps,
The world's a place of booby-traps,
Where once you had been bolder.

Another scene
Is when you think about What Might have Been,
Forgetful that
What Might Have Been is where you were just at.

Be then content
That you've enough to pay the rent,
Take pleasure in those joys that still abound,
That nowadays the rose blooms all year round.

TIME UNTITLED

Too swift the past is dust,
Ashes and rust,
Not even epilogue,
But lush compost,
A fallen log
On earth through which too many roots have passed.

What's now
And so alive beneath the sun
And so immediately keen,
How soon its time allow is run:
All that ado -
And me and you -
And then it's all as if had never been.

That bead
Of sweat was once a seed
That passed through a bird-gut,
Became a tree
That lived a thousand years,
Only to be
Felled for someone's need,
No if or but.
That someone's house burned down,
To tears
And brief appal,
Then all were gone
As if had never lived and loved at all.

ADVANCING AGE

When I am near my end
And have become your niddle-noddle friend,
The one who finds it difficult to bend
Or straighten, harder yet to wend
His weary way from bed to bath to tend
To everyday affairs, will you still lend
Your love, respect, make possible to mend
Our little differences, nor fail to send
Your greetings and take trouble to attend
Dull teas and tantrums, so as not offend?
And when at last my time comes to ascend,
Will your heart rend?
I fear 'twould buck the trend.
Maybe my crusty Will I should amend!

ANCIEN RÉGIME

Ever sat on the pot
And let thought meander,
Let memory wander,
Then can't remember
Whether you've 'been' or not?

I can still walk a mile,
Can still cross a stile
And I still scrub up well
For a dance with a belle.
Don't think that I can quite keep pace
With Internet and Cyberspace,
But bar softening brain
I hope to maintain
Facility as a bit of a rhymer,
Deferring acquaintance with Doctor Alzheimer.

AMBULANCE

Dear God,
I've been involved in a terrible Accident
Called Life.
I woke up in a hospital named Earth,
Where everyone's a patient,
Even the staff. Please - do not laugh!

The grounds are very nice
And everyone assures me
I'll be home in a trice,
None the worse in appearance
For the experience,
And as soon as my wound mends
Be back with all my family and friends.

EPITAPH

I've fed friend,
Fish
And bird of the air,
People for whom I did not care
And flower
And tree
That meant much more to me.

It is my wish,
Therefore,
When I am past my hour
And at my end,
In forest, field
And rolling weald,
Ocean, brook,
At the road bend,
In crowd
And cloud,
That you and your
Should come and look:

You'll find me there.

As I close these pages, I reflect on why it should be that, so late in life, I seem to have 'found my voice' - one answerable, that is, to no earthly master - and although it may be of significance and the work of value to nobody but myself, verse pours from me daily as never before.

But I seem often to be writing for someone else to set to music. My youth was sadly starved of musical education and I have no alternative but employ such skill as a beneficent Creator thought fit to bestow and which, as St. Paul exhorted in his letter to the Corinthians, I must need 'covet earnestly', being short of any other available means of expression or utterance.

With a book of Choral Latin as my guide, I reproduce below what must be my final addition to the present collection: a Mass rendered into English verse which I hope is not too far adrift from what is counted invariable in that superior form of worship. I wrote the first draft at one go, while sitting under a succession of shady trees on a hot July day in Kew Gardens. I was unexpectedly joined in a quiet glade there by a glorious peacock, who presented himself in full, proud and lustrous feather. We chatted amicably for a while, and he brought some influence to bear upon my thinking. I humbly dedicate the result to the incomparable Choir of St. Paul's Cathedral, which has afforded me many uplifting hours of superlative choral music.

AN ENGLISH MASS: *THE PEACOCK*

Kyrie

Merciful, benign,
Omnipotent, divine,
O God let Thy great mercy upon us shine.

Gloria

Glory to God
The Creator
Who maketh green the earth and brings
The spring,
Who breatheth life,
Renewing everything.
God of universal Mind,
Forgive our strife:
Look kindly upon our so unworthy kind.
Protect
All that walk or swim or fly
In colour and content
From our neglect,

That they be not rent
Or die,
Bird, beast or fish
Let be as you would wish.
Nor, pray you, cease to sow
All wondrous things that grow
Nor fail to send
The sun and rain,
Your bounty without end
Renewing earth again.
Your bread we eat,
Your wine we sip,
Earth is Thy Holy Seat,
Ours the stewardship.

We have praised
Not least
He whom you raised
Your Son
To be the Holy One
And sent
Yourself to represent
And bring as feast
All your great worth
To see
And be
Here with us, God on earth.

Our Lord who
Came to do
Great miracles. His message first unfurl'd
That told us how to live in this lovely world.
Mercy upon all those of us who fail'd
To recognise Him, left his life unhail'd,
Although His sacrifice
Brought us redemption from what sins entice.
Our debt remit:
To share Christ's suffering,
Not add to it.

Receive our prayer as we
Cry Glory to the Trinity:
God, the Son, the Holy Ghost
And all the Host.

Glory to God on High
The One and Only,
Bless us and be
Compassionate to we
Who here so lonely
Live and die,
Though Eden is our land, Heaven our sky.

Credo

I believe
In God the Father Almighty,
Lord of the Seen and Unseen,
Of now, of all to come and all that's been,
Both near and far
From Earth to Heaven's most distant star,
All life and all Creation,
From Earth to Heaven's most distant constellation.
Let there be, therefore,
All praise to His eternal Glory,
God of Light,
Whose Son came down from Heaven within His sight,
One with the Father,
Holy, incarnate,
In state of Grace,
Born of Mary,
Of human face,
Lived for us all and died,
Being crucified,
And from His pain
Redemption came and hope of life again.

I believe
In Thou for Whom Time dared no history,
Granted our Christian mystery.
I believe in Heaven,
In Holy Mother Church
And remission of sin,
That I may rise as one with Christ,
Forgiven
And at Heaven's gate let in.

Sanctus with Benedictus

Bless us, O Lord,
Who knows our pain,
Who standeth by
And is there
When he hears our cry,
Heeds our prayer
And, knowing everything,
Hears us when we weep and when we sing.

Lord God of Hosts,
Whose Glory and Holiness
Pervades all Heaven and earth and every place,
Who comes to bless?
He hath seen God's Face
Who blessèd cometh in the name of Grace.

Agnus Dei

Lamb of God,
Who showeth mercy,
Remove all sin,
Without and within,
And grant us lease
Of Thine eternal peace.

INDEX OF FIRST LINES

101